ALL THINGS HEDGEHOGS FOR KIDS

FILLED WITH PLENTY OF FACTS, PHOTOS, AND FUN TO LEARN ALL ABOUT HEDGEHOGS

ANIMAL READS

WWW.ANIMALREADS.COM

THIS BOOK BELONGS TO...

_____

_____

WWW.ANIMALREADS.COM

CONTENTS

Say Hello to Our Spikey Little Friends!	1
What is a Hedgehog?	5
Different Species of Hedgehogs	13
Characteristics & Appearance	21
A History of Hedgehogs	45
The Life Cycle of a Hedgehog	49
Awesome Facts About Hedgehogs	57
Help the Spikes!	61
Thank You!	69

SAY HELLO TO OUR SPIKEY LITTLE FRIENDS!

Hedgehogs are pretty interesting looking creatures, right? They have adorable faces with small button-like noses and eyes. And what about all those spikes! Cartoons and children's stories always feature plenty of cute and adventurous features about these little crawlers.

But did you know real hedgehogs are actually pretty slow? They are less likely to zip by you than to shuffle along happily, looking for some lunch. It might also surprise you that they can actually be pretty loud and clumsy as they crawl around leaves and shrubs looking for something to eat.

There are so many fun facts about real-life hedgehogs to learn!

Did you know that hedgehogs have survived, almost unchanged, for 15 MILLION years? **WOWzers!**

Or that hedgehogs sleep for 7 months straight every year?!

So, forget everything you think you might already know about these spikey little guys and gals...

Let's check out the amazing (*and true*) world of the hedgehog.

THIS WILL

SPIKE

YOUR INTEREST!

WHAT IS A HEDGEHOG?

Hedgehogs are small mammals with spiky quills. They are members of the order known as *Eulypotyphla*, which translates to "**truly fat and blind.**" While not the most flattering of names for a mammal order, the group also includes moon rats (*who aren't rodents*), moles, and shrews. Shrews are insectivores and are very closely related to hedgehogs, who also eat a diet mostly of bugs. Under the order Eulypotyphla, hedgehogs are in the family called Erinaceidae.

WHERE DO HEDGEHOGS LIVE?

In the wild, hedgehogs are found in many different kinds of terrain. Hedgehogs live and thrive in woodlands, grasslands, deserts, mountainous areas, and even Mediterranean vineyards. They wander through moors and marshes and African savannas. Different species have adapted to each of these different environments.

Did you know hedgehogs even might live in your backyard? **That's right!**

Hedgehogs, like raccoons, opossums, deer, and others, have adapted themselves to share spaces with people. While hedgehogs can still be found in the country shuffling along through the woods, they are also found wandering through big city parks.

Some things in cities actually help hedgehogs, who are always looking for an easy meal. Streetlights draw many insects to their bright glow. When the bugs get tired, they slip to the ground and become a ready-made feast for a happily waiting hedgehog.

HEDGEHOGS VS. PORCUPINES - AREN'T THEY REALLY THE SAME THING?

People often get hedgehogs and porcupines mixed up. *After all, they are both small spikey mammals, right? How different can they be?*

There are actually lots of differences between hedgehogs and porcupines!

One big difference has to do with their spines or quills. Porcupines, unlike hedgehogs, can shoot out their sharp quills when in danger. They also have a lot more quills, almost 30,000! Hedgehogs only have around 5,000 spines. The length of the quills is another difference between the two animals. While porcupines have 2-to-3-inch quills, hedgehog quills are only about 1 inch long.

But that isn't the only thing different about these two spikey creatures. Porcupines are much larger than hedgehogs. Hedgehogs range in size from 4 to 12 inches in length and around 5 to 56 ounces in weight. On the contrary, porcupines can be 25 to 36 inches long and around 10 to 28 pounds. **That's quite a difference!**

Hedgehogs also don't live as long as porcupines. Hedgehogs have an average life span of about 3 to 8 years. Porcupines, however, can live up to 27 years. Porcupines also live in North America in the wild, whereas hedgehogs are found in Europe and Africa.

Lastly, the diets of these two animals are very different. As you will soon learn, hedgehogs are **omnivores** and eat a wide variety of plants, fruits, fungi, eggs, reptiles, and insects. On the other hand, porcupines are strict **herbivores**, which means they only eat plants.

LIVING ON THE HEDGE!

DIFFERENT SPECIES OF HEDGEHOGS

Did you know that hedgehogs come in many varieties? Some are big, and some are little. Some have large ears, and some have almost no visible ears at all. Some live in Siberia, and others live in the sweltering deserts of Africa!

Let's learn about the amazing species of hedgehogs that make up this fascinating group of animals.

EUROPEAN HEDGEHOG

Also known as *Erinaceus europaeus* and the "common" hedgehog, the European hedgehog is widely found in European countries such as France, Italy, Spain, the United Kingdom, and others.

These brown and black hedgehogs are the largest of all the species and can grow 10 inches long and weigh over 2.4 lbs. Docile and easygoing, these hedgehogs are often found poking along a garden fence or shuffling along for bugs on the forest floor. Once quite abundant in Great Britain, there are less than a million left there today.

SOUTHERN WHITE-BREASTED HEDGEHOG

The southern white-breasted hedgehog, also known as *Erinaceus concolor*, is nearly identical to the European hedgehog. *The only difference?* A white spot on its chest. For years, these species were thought to be the same thing. But now we know they are their own group altogether. These little guys and girls cover quite a lot of territory and are found in Eastern Europe all the way to Western Asia.

NORTHERN WHITE-BREASTED HEDGEHOG

Like its southern friend, the northern white-breasted hedgehog, or *Erinaceus roumanicus*, is also found throughout a wide area. This hedgehog can be found in Siberia, all the way over to Poland, and down to Greece. Thankfully, there is still a healthy population of this species in the wild. It has a white mark on its chest as well, but also a slightly differently shaped jaw from the European hedgehog and the southern white-breasted hedgehog.

DESERT HEDGEHOG

The desert hedgehog, or *Paraechinus aethiopicus*, is a small but mighty species. Living in the deserts of the Middle East and even parts of North Africa, this hedgehog has special kidneys that allow them to go long distances without water. One of the tiniest of all hedgehog species, the desert hedgehog only grows to about 6 to 8 inches. They have a long face, light tan fur on their stomach and face, and brown fur on top with light-colored quills. They look a little different than their hedgehog cousins and stand out with their large pointy ears. Desert hedgehogs eat lizards, insects, and even scorpions! In order not to be stung by the scorpion's poison, the hedgehog bites off the stinger first and discards it.

AFRICAN PYGMY HEDGEHOG/FOUR-TOED HEDGEHOG

The African Pygmy Hedgehog, also known as *Atelerix albiventris*, is one of the most common hedgehogs known today. They often have a dark face, darker back fur, and a very light cream-colored underside. They are found all over Africa, particularly in the central and eastern areas.

Ever adaptable, these little hedgehogs can be found living in fields among crops, wandering through grasslands, hunting for insects on the savanna, and even poking along into city gardens. This species is the most common kind of hedgehog to be kept and sold as pets. At only around 8 to 10 inches long, they are very tiny and adorable. They are also very playful and active and like to swim.

I'M SO GLAD YOU

PRICKED ME!

CHARACTERISTICS & APPEARANCE

The most recognizable thing about hedgehogs is, of course, their hair or spines. These spiky hairs always give the hedgehog a look as if it just rolled out of bed. These spiky quills are actually hollow hairs stiff with *keratin*. Keratin is the protein that is found in your hair and nails. The keratin makes the hair stiff and pokey. These pokey quills actually have a pretty important job.

What do you do when you are frightened—scream, run away, jump? Hedgehogs can't scream, aren't built to jump very well, and they also can't run very fast. Despite their famous blue mascot, hedgehogs are actually quite slow.

They can run up to 4.5 miles an hour but only for a short distance at a time. When chased, a hedgehog might be able to get up to 6 miles per hour. Just to compare, an average person walks about 3-4 miles an hour.

That means you could probably outrun a hedgehog just by walking!

So, if hedgehogs can't depend on speed to get away from predators, what can they do? When a hedgehog feels scared or threatened, it curls up into a tight ball.

By doing this, the stiff spines on its body point outwards and provide a defense. Think about it. If you were an animal like a coyote or wolf and wanted a tasty hedgehog snack, would you want to bite down on something sharp and pokey? No way!

One sign of danger and a hedgehog can roll into a tight ball of sharp pricklers and be protected.

Another interesting fact about hedgehogs is the sounds they make. Hedgehogs talk to each other with a combination of different sounds, including grunts, squeals, and snuffles. Hedgehogs live on their own and don't get a chance to talk with many other hedgehogs. However, all those sounds are pretty important during mating season when hedgehogs are looking to pair up.

Like a lot of small mammals, hedgehogs are **nocturnal**, which means they come out and are active at night and sleep during the day. However, during spring, when hedgehogs have just come out of **hibernation**, you might also see some during the day. **Hibernating** is when animals like hedgehogs, bears, and bats sleep for months and have minimal activity to survive the long cold winters of their habitats. We will learn more about how hedgehogs go about this process a little later, but hibernating takes a lot of energy, and newly-awake hedgehogs are eager to find food.

Finding food is job number one for hedgehogs! Hedgehogs use their sense of smell to guide them to food. Shuffling along, looking for something to fill their ever-empty bellies, is what hedgehogs do best.

WHAT DO HEDGEHOGS EAT?

Hedgehogs are **omnivores**. Omnivores are animals that eat meat and plants. And hedgehogs, especially, are omnivores that love eating insects. They are happiest when they get to snuffle along and look for tasty bugs.

So, what's on the menu at the Hedgehog Café? **Let's take a look!**

Hedgehogs love to eat the following foods:

- **Bugs** – invertebrates (*animals that don't have a spine or backbone*) make up the biggest part of a hedgehog's diet. They love to eat worms, slugs, beetles, caterpillars, earwigs, millipedes, and other insects.

- **Things that hop and slither** – Reptiles and Amphibians are also part of a happy hedgehog lunch. Toads, frogs, and small snakes are all fair game for a snack.
- **Small rodents and birds** – Hedgehogs will eat baby rodents (*like mice and rats*), baby birds, and bird eggs (*if they stumble upon a ground bird's nest*).
- **Veggie buffet** – Don't forget the plants! Hedgehogs are big fans of grass roots, berries, melons, and watermelons. They will also eat fungi, such as wild mushrooms.
- **Carrion** – Carrion is the remains of dead animals. Hedgehogs help clean up the forest by eating the dead animals they find.

Did you find anything you would eat at the Hedgehog Café? How about a nice caterpillar sandwich? Or a snake salad? **Or maybe you'll just want to stick to some melon!**

You may be wondering how hedgehogs break into the hard shells of invertebrate bugs like beetles? After all, crunching up a beetle isn't the easiest thing in the world. However, hedgehogs have no problem cracking into insect shells because of their needle-sharp teeth.

WHAT SHOULD PET HEDGEHOGS EAT?

Hedgehogs that live as pets are fed a little differently. It would be challenging to feed a hedgehog a wide variety of bugs like it would get in the wild. For this reason, hedgehog owners feed their pets a base food, such as a good quality cat kibble, and then add other kinds of food. Unlike a cat or dog that can do well with just one type of food, hedgehogs have a stomach that can and should have a lot of variety. After all, it's rare that a wild hedgehog would only eat worms or only eat beetles.

For the healthiest hedgehog, owners feed them a few kinds of kibble to keep the food interesting and varied. Then they also add berries, green leafy veggies, and some live insects.

Hedgehog pets usually get crickets or grasshoppers. However, insects are higher in fat, and pet hedgehogs can quickly become overweight since they aren't traveling as much as they would be in the wild. Owners should never feed their hedgehog wild insects as they might have parasites or other issues that can make a pet hedgehog sick.

Why are hedgehogs always so hungry? Hedgehogs in the wild are always busy eating, eating, and eating! Since they need to chunk up for the winter months when they hibernate, they are always eager to find the next meal.

HIBERNATION

Some species survive the cold winter months when food isn't available by hibernating. This means the animals fall into a deep sleep and burrow into a den to spend the entire winter there. Bears and even butterflies are examples of animals that hibernate, and hedgehogs are also hibernators. And, like others in this group, they are busy all autumn **eating, eating, and eating!**

After all, it's not like they get to wake up for mid-winter snacks throughout the season. Hibernating animals must put on enough weight and body fat to give them the energy to survive the long sleep.

When the temperature starts to drop to 38 degrees and lower, hedgehogs begin to get sleepy. This is their body's way of preparing them to sleep when the year grows colder. But late autumn and early winter can be a dangerous time of year for hedgehogs.

Hedgehogs will take short snoozes on these cold nights. But if the temperature drops further or doesn't rise again before the hedgehog has found a safe, warm shelter, it is vulnerable to freezing to death.

Hedgehogs must find shelter before they get too sleepy. Hedgehogs typically don't dig their own holes but rather find empty holes to build their nests in. They will line it with leaves and make sure it is insulated and warm.

Once a hedgehog has created a safe and warm home to ride out the cold winter months, it can settle down into a deep sleep. The hedgehog will sleep from the end of October until early April.

You may be wondering how a hedgehog can survive eating nothing for almost seven months? Hedgehogs have an amazing ability to slow down their body rhythms and metabolism. This allows them to use less of their stored energy during hibernation. While a hedgehog's heart usually beats at about 170 beats per minute, their heart rate will slow down to an incredible 5 beats per minute in winter sleep!

Hedgehogs don't set alarms or look at the calendar to know when to wake up. Just like the cooling temperatures make the hedgehog sleepy, the warming temperatures tell the hedgehog when it is time to wake up. This cues the hedgehog to release hormones that tell its body to return to normal.

Once awake, the hedgehog is hungry! They would have lost 40% of their weight and strength from that long nap. The hedgehog will immediately set out looking for food and water. It is not uncommon to see hedgehogs out during the day in spring, even though they are nocturnal. This is because they need to hunt and eat more to build back up their lost weight. Hedgehogs also wake up super thirsty. **Imagine if you didn't drink anything for half the year!** *We bet you would be thirsty too.*

You may be wondering if all hedgehogs hibernate? And the answer is nope. Hedgehogs that don't live in snowy places with distinct seasons of spring, summer, fall, and winter don't need to hibernate. Desert hedgehogs in Africa don't need to sleep half the year away because there is no long cold season.

Spring can be a difficult time for hedgehogs. If the cold suddenly comes back with more snow, hedgehogs can be in danger of freezing again since they will have already left their nest. Once they leave their nest, they won't usually return to it. Fortunately, most of the time, it doesn't get too cold again for them.

For the most part, cold weather is the least of a hedgehog's worries. Unfortunately, the world does offer traps they have to avoid.

PREDATORS AND DANGER

Even with sharp quills for protection, hedgehogs can still run into trouble. Several animals would like nothing more than a tasty hedgehog snack.

In England, the European badger is the most dangerous predator for European hedgehogs. Although badgers are also fond of insects and plants, they don't mind adding hedgehogs to their regular diet.

Hedgehogs are also a favorite treat of eagle owls. These large birds of prey hunt small mammals in the dark. Their large eyes give them excellent night vision. Young hedgehogs are often caught unaware by predators like the eagle owl.

Beech Martins are another danger for hedgehogs as they wander around at night. But here, the hedgehogs' spikey defense can often successfully keep these weasel-like predators away.

The Common European Adder is a poisonous snake that isn't exactly a predator to Hedgehogs. Hedgehogs eat snakes, but going after an Adder can be tricky business. Adders will attack if feeling threatened. The hedgehog is protected from the snake's bite by hiding behind its shield of prickles. However, if the snake manages to bite the face or underside of a hedgehog, it would die from its poison.

Probably the biggest threat to hedgehogs today is traffic and cars. Hedgehogs can't read "Do Not Cross" signs or use sidewalks. Hedgehogs follow their noses, looking for food. Unfortunately, this can mean that hedgehogs, with their slow reactions, often get hit by cars.

Sometimes mother hedgehogs die, and that is especially sad. However, wildlife rescuers try to help orphan baby hedgehogs, who can sometimes be nursed on formula and helped survive.

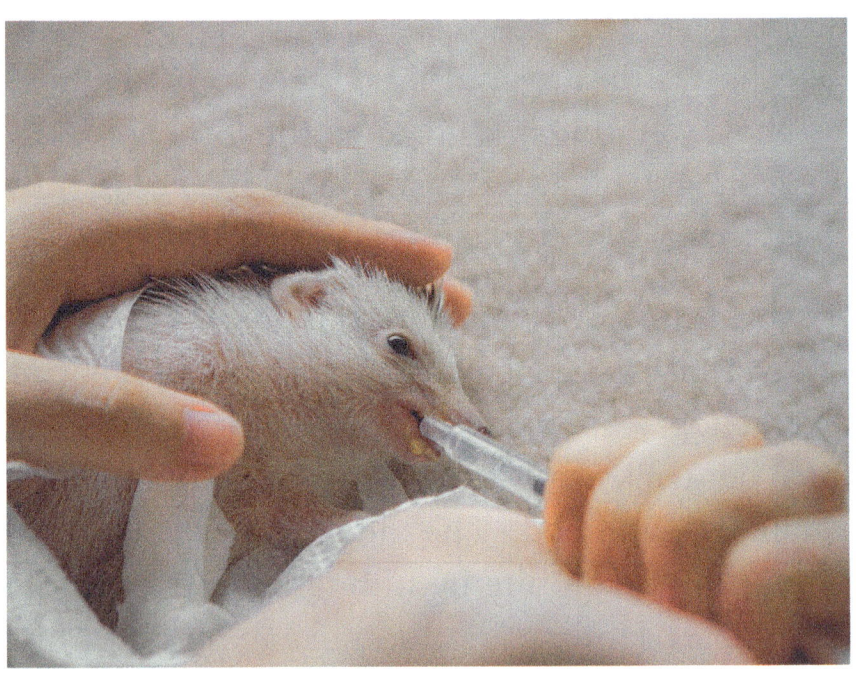

Water can cause other dangerous situations for hedgehogs. Summer rains can cause flooding, and hedgehogs can quickly be caught in the downpour. While hedgehogs can swim, they tire out quickly. It's important for hedgehogs to not get caught up in a current and kept away from the shore, or they can drown.

WHAT DO YOU CALL A HEDGEHOG THAT DOESN'T EAT WORMS?

A HEDGE-atarian!

A HISTORY OF HEDGEHOGS

Imagine a time when saber-toothed tigers and mastodons roamed, crashing through giant ferns and prehistoric plants. *Do you know how else would be there?*

Hedgehogs!

We know what you're thinking... "*But huge, ferocious hedgehogs with massive spines then, right?*"

Nope! Just hedgehogs.

In fact, hedgehogs have been around for 15 million years and have pretty much looked the same the entire time. Same cute little face. Same spikey hair.

Except for the Mediterranean hedgehog that was about the size of a pig and didn't last that long, the hedgehog has been relatively unevolved all this time.

Scientists guess that the hedgehog is just very well-adapted for its life and hasn't needed to undergo big changes. Hedgehogs are one of the oldest living mammals on earth today. Pretty cool, huh!

WHAT SOUNDS DO HEDGEHOGS MAKE WHEN THEY KISS?

OUCH!

THE LIFE CYCLE OF A HEDGEHOG

Hedgehogs are solitary, which means they prefer to live alone. However, hedgehogs will look for others of their kind in the spring. Spring is the time of year when hedgehogs are looking for a mate. Once a female and male hedgehog find each other, they start the mating process, also known as the *"hedgehog carousel."*

The male will circle around the female several times. She often turns her spiky shoulder to him if he moves in too fast. It can take a few hours before a successful mating process can happen. Once it is done, the male goes on his way to look for other females who are also fertile. In one night, a male hedgehog can go on to mate with several females. After the mating process, male hedgehogs are not involved in raising their young.

After 3 weeks, the female will be ready to give birth in a couple of weeks. She will then start looking for a safe place and prepare it to be ready for her young. A female will have just 1 litter of babies a year. Any kind of hidden shelter will do for a nest, such as a pile of leaves or a stack of wood. Another option is a leftover hole or nest from another animal.

At around 4-6 weeks, the babies are born. Hedgehogs usually have 5-6 babies in each litter. A baby hedgehog is called a "**hoglet**." When they are born, the hoglets have flat spikes stuck to their skin, so they don't hurt their mother when being born. But after just a few hours pass, the hoglet spikes will stick up.

After a few days, these birth spikes fall out, and larger spikes take their place. Like most mammals, hoglets survive on just their mother's milk for the first weeks. The mother has to go out to get food and water to keep up her own strength and milk supply.

The hoglets stick close together, sleeping and keeping each other warm. As newborns, they still can't see or walk well just yet. The hoglets turn into rambunctious teenagers in just a few weeks, though.

After around 3 ½ weeks, they can leave the nest to venture out into the brand-new world on small outings with their mother. At this point, they look just like adult hedgehogs, only smaller. They even have a full set of adult teeth!

Right away, the hedgehog kids are off and running, smelling this and climbing that! **The mother hedgehog has her hands full for sure!** It's still her job to lead these little outings and keep everyone safe and together. The hoglets also want to follow their mother, after all, anytime they are hungry or cold, they can snuggle up to their mother and get a drink of milk or a cuddle. These young hoglets are still quite easily chilled, so warming up to mom is also important for staying healthy and strong. The outings are important as the mother teaches her young how to hunt and get by in the real world.

As the hoglets keep growing, they soon run out of room under their mother. Around this time, the mother's milk slows up and stops. This is also a cue to the mother that her children are ready to be left on their own. As she wanders off, the hedgehog kids are now ready to go out and find their own way.

They will each go find their own areas to hunt and explore, such as a meadow or forest. Since hedgehogs live alone in the wild, they don't mind this quiet life on their own.

When the hoglets are full-grown, they will find their own mate next spring and raise a new litter of their own.

YOU'RE LOOKIN'

SHARP!

AWESOME FACTS ABOUT HEDGEHOGS

DID YOU KNOW?

- The Middle English word for hedgehog is heyghoge. Other names for hedgehogs are hedgepig and furze-pig. A Furze is a type of spiny, thorny shrub. Hmm… wonder why they thought the hedgehog looked like that bush?

- Every spikey hair on a hedgehog, all 5,000, get replaced every single year!

- Hedgehogs have long faces and snouts compared to their rounder bodies to help them forage for everything they enjoy munching on. Their face shape helps them hunt and look for fruit under leaves.

- Despite how slow they move around, hedgehogs actually travel quite far every night. They can travel about 2 miles in an evening, which is a lot for those tiny steps they take.

- Hedgehogs are lactose intolerant. Besides the milk they get from their moms, or special formula rescue organizations give hoglets, water is all they need.

WHAT DID THE HEDGEHOG SAY TO THE CACTUS?

"Brother!?"

HELP THE SPIKES!

We hope you have enjoyed learning all about these prickly food-loving animals. Hedgehogs may not be as endangered as tigers or pandas, but they still need your help. In the United Kingdom, where wild hedgehogs are common, there used to be around 30 million in the 1950s and 60s. Today, scientists think there may be only a little less than 1 million hedgehogs left.

There are lots of problems facing hedgehogs today. Loss of habitat is one of the biggest. Too many natural areas are crisscrossed with roads and highways. Since hedgehogs aren't fast, crossing highways safely is a big problem for sure.

Pesticide use is another thing that hurts hedgehogs. Not only are the chemicals bad for our spikey friends, but when we kill insects, it has a big impact on the animals that rely on those insects as their primary source of food.

HOW YOU CAN HELP

If you live in a place with wild hedgehogs, here are a few practical and easy ways you can help them.

MAKE BACKYARD PONDS SAFE

Although ponds and deep fountains can be beautiful, they can be dangerous for hedgehogs. Even though hedgehogs can swim, they will quickly tire and drown if they fall into a pool of water and can't climb back out again. Make your pond safe by putting in a small board ramp or by creating gently sloping edges that a hedgehog can easily use to climb out with if it falls in the water.

CREATE A HEDGEHOG DOOR

Another easy way to help hedgehogs is to create a small hole in the bottom of garden fences. Hedgehogs travel quite a distance every night and need to cover a lot of territory to fill themselves up on insects. Creating little passageways for hedgehogs to easily travel from area to area allows hedgehogs to shuffle along uninterrupted and away from the dangers of roads.

MAKE A HEDGEHOG REST-STOP

You may find a few hedgehogs traveling through your garden or yard from time to time. With the help of an adult, you can set up a hedgehog rest-stop during autumn, when hedgehogs are trying to pack on the weight for their long winter sleep. Put out a little dish of water, prop up a board or two for shelter, and set out a little food. Hedgehogs can eat wet, meaty dog or cat food, unsalted peanuts, or you can even buy hedgehog food online. Some things to avoid are fish-flavored cat food, mealworms, and milk or dairy. Hedgehogs are lactose intolerant and will get a stomach ache.

PLANTING FLOWERS HELPS TOO

Another simple thing you can do to help hedgehogs and attract them to your garden is by planting diverse wildflowers. Wildflowers attract various insects, which you know hedgehogs love to eat.

MAKE A BEETLE BUFFET

As beetles are an important part of a hedgehog's autumn diet (*making up almost half of all they eat*), why not help encourage beetles too? Stacking logs or piling up areas where wood can decompose will help create a nice beetle buffet for hedgehogs. Compost piles are another fantastic way to encourage a healthy ecosystem of bugs and wildlife in your backyard.

LOVE AT FIRST SPIKE!

THANK YOU!

Thank you for reading this book and for allowing us to share our love for hedgehogs with you!

If you've enjoyed this book, please let us know by leaving a rating and a brief review wherever you made your purchase! This helps us spread the word to other readers!

Thank you for your time, and have an awesome day!

For more information, please visit:

www.animalreads.com

SENDING YOU SOME

HEDGEHUGS!

© Copyright 2022 - All rights reserved Admore Publishing

ISBN: 978-3-96772-127-0

ISBN: 978-3-96772-128-7

Animal Reads at www.animalreads.com

The content contained within this book may not be reproduced, duplicated or transmitted without direct written permission from the author or the publisher.

Under no circumstances will any blame or legal responsibility be held against the publisher, or author, for any damages, reparation, or monetary loss due to the information contained within this book. Either directly or indirectly.

Published by Admore Publishing: Gotenstraße, Berlin, Germany

www.admorepublishing.com

Made in the USA
Las Vegas, NV
08 March 2023